THEPOETICUNDERGROUND

voyage

ISBN 978-1-326-06080-0

thepoeticunderground.com

For all the voyagers.

thepoeticunderground.com

CONTENTS

Winter Wonders

Do you remember the night the moon dropped from the sky?
And we ran through the forest to find where it lie,
I was tripping on tree roots and slipping on snow,
You were holding my hand saying not to let go,
When we found it at last there were twigs in our hair,
A rose on our cheeks and our breath in the air,
And the words to describe it got caught in our throats,
As its silver light danced through the threads of our coats,
We knew that our eyes had not seen such a view,
You were looking at it,
I was looking at you.

~e.h

Wanderer

You're packing up your sleeping bag,
Your lantern and your tent,
And you're off to find the life you lost,
But you're not sure where it went,
And I hope those mountains teach you,
How to stand both tall and proud,
That you see your life much clearer,
With your head above the cloud,
I hope you swim through rivers,
With their currents swift and fast,
That they show you must be careful,
When you wash away your past,
I hope that you are humbled,
By the vastness of the sea,
That the eagles high above you,
Make you feel like you are free,
I hope when night has fallen,
And your fire's just a spark,
That the stars shine to remind you,
That there's beauty in the dark,
But most of all I'm hoping,
That you're learning while you roam,
That no matter the distance,
You can always come back home.

~e.h

Her Great Escape

They say it's ten years to the day,
Since she disappeared from sight,
Packed up her best intentions,
And ran away into the night,
That the pine trees on the hillside,
Are still heard calling her name,
And the wind whistles with woe,
Trying to find someone to blame,
But despite its howling fury,
There is no one here at fault,
For the world was just a piece,
Inside her restless soul's revolt,
And like you can't define the ocean,
By the parts that reach the sand,
Perhaps she was much deeper,
Than our minds could understand,
So legend tells the story,
Of how she left no trace to track,
That she escaped this bitter earth,
Across a silver moonbeam's back,
And if you ever wake at night,
To moonlight splashed across your face,
It is her hand reaching for yours,
Her very own cosmic embrace.

~e.h

Petals and Promises

She was the summer's last sunflower,
Writing a letter to July,
As though one final correspondence,
Would make an easier goodbye,
But already she could feel them,
The approaching winds of change,
An autumn she would never see,
Both beautiful and strange,
As the heat's embrace got softer,
She watched the leaves all fall and settle,
And had one last look for love,
Within her few remaining petals,
But though the sun had made a promise,
She knew it was one that he forgot,
As her final petal fell to earth,
He loves me,
He loves me not.

~e.h

She was a shooting star,
Her smile so bright and rare,
That by the time that you had blinked,
There was no sign it had been there.

~e.h

Winter Wind

She's the ever-changing winter wind,
A gust of clean crisp air,
Roaring through the living room,
And tousling up your hair,
She whistles through the doorways,
As she sails right down the hall,
Dancing through the golden leaves,
That mark the end of fall,
But like the frozen winter wind,
She bends to no one's will,
Some days she is a hurricane,
And other days she's still,
There's moments when her laughter,
Could give flight to paper planes,
But her silence can convince you,
Trees will never sway again,
She'll push the clouds out of the sky,
And stir the wildest seas,
But no matter how you know her,
You cannot predict her breeze,
There's days when you'll feel foolish,
For the scarf wrapped round your throat,
But with her there is no knowing,
When you ought to wear a coat.

~e.h

The Paperback Princess

She smelled of books and stories,
Of all the worlds she'd lived within,
As though the ink had left the pages,
To find a new home in her skin,
She didn't quite belong here,
Lived a life within her head,
Like she'd slipped out from the covers,
Of a paperback instead,
And you'd see it in her eyes,
That they were deeper than a well,
She was a whole library of stories,
That we'd beg of her to tell,
When she spoke the world would listen,
To the adventures of her mind,
For if there's such a thing as magic,
Then it was something she could find,
And her heart had looked much further,
Than her eyes had ever seen,
She'd walked on words to places,
Her two feet had never been,
It's years now since she moved,
And we all failed to keep in touch,
So her memory's all faded,
Like a book you've read too much,
But if she hoped to leave us ink-stained,
She should know she did succeed,
For even now we all still look for her,
In every book we read.

~e.h

The Abandoned Heart Hotel

Inside her ribcage city,
Lies an abandoned heart hotel,
Haunted with the memories,
Of a time it once knew well,
If you're quiet and imagine,
You can hear the closing doors,
The forgotten conversations,
And the footsteps on the floors,
It was open many years ago,
When she was still young and naïve,
Believing if she gave enough,
She'd eventually receive,
Each day she cleaned and cooked,
To ensure comfort for her guests,
But as people kept arriving,
It grew heavy in her chest,
Eventually to hear herself,
She almost had to shout,
Over the people who had once moved in,
And then never moved out,
Although they'd faded from her life,
Their memories roamed the halls,
For she was so afraid of heartbreak,
That she clung onto them all,
But hotels aren't designed,
For everyone who comes, to stay,
And when you keep on cramming people in,

Something's going to give way,
And so the story goes,
Her heart hotel slowly closed down,
She learnt to let things go,
And moved in to a nicer town,
That she's doing so much better,
And she owns a cottage now,
Where the ones she loves the dearest,
Are the only guests she will allow.

~e.h

Windows

You thought her eyes were a window,
In the room that housed her soul,
And the things you saw behind it,
Made you think she'd make you whole,
So you started throwing pebbles,
Begging her to let you in,
Until the signs of your affection,
Appeared as bruises on her skin,
But what you'd failed to notice,
Was that her curtains were drawn tight,
And the promises you thought you'd seen,
Were just tricks of the light,
She'd become just a reflection,
Of who you wished that she would be,
With a life to make yours better,
And perfect personality,
So when her window shattered,
And you peered into her room,
You found a very different person,
To the one that you'd assumed,
And I hope you begged forgiveness,
For the glass left on her floor,
And for thinking that a person,
Owed it to you to be much more.

~e.h

I'll plant a row of daisy seeds,
In the space below each eye,
So they'll remind you of your beauty,
When they bloom each time you cry.

~e.h

Darkness

You dipped your toes into the darkness,
As though to test if it was cold,
And I knew right when you shivered,
You were more scared than you had told,
I wrote my words into a life ring,
Something to keep your world afloat,
But against the strength of your nightmare,
They were a soggy paper boat,
I don't know what the blackness told you,
What wondrous things it planned to give,
But I watched as the light died in your eyes,
Along with your will to live,
I screamed your name to pierce the silence,
But you were too long gone to hear,
Caught somewhere between being noticed,
And wanting to disappear,
You once said you were scared of darkness,
And that you'd never learnt to swim,
But with its promises pumped through your veins,
You held your breath and jumped right in.

~e.h

My World Within

How can you say you know me,
When you've only seen my skin,
And not the untamed world I hide,
That's growing deep within?
You haven't heard my ribs all creak,
Behind each plaited vine,
Or swum beneath the waterfall,
That cascades down my spine,
You've not been here for long enough,
To watch a new life start,
Or find the run-down castle,
Lying just inside my heart,
You haven't climbed the branches,
That are wrapped around each lung,
Swaying with the breezes,
That come dancing past my tongue,
Don't mark me with your footprints,
If you plan to leave too soon,
And only want to know me,
When my plants are all in bloom,
Because the birdsong might be pretty,
But it's not for you they sing,
And if you think my winter is too cold,
You don't deserve my spring.

~e.h

The Cardboard Kingdom

You tied a string around my heart,
So that it wouldn't drift away,
As we soared above the trees,
Watching our kingdom turn to day,
You were the bravest tin-foil knight,
Our cardboard world had ever seen,
And with a crown of twisted clovers,
I was the impish forest queen,
We scratched our names across the skyline,
Playing hopscotch on the stars,
Collecting drops of golden sunlight,
In our treasured crystal jars,
And I thought we'd live forever,
In the kingdom that we owned,
Still dancing with its trees,
Even after we had grown,
But I learnt there's no forever,
So much magic cannot last,
When you ripped your tin-foil armour,
And crammed it all into your past,
I clung onto that kingdom,
Until my arms were numb with pain,
But cardboard worlds grow soggy,
When they're left out in the rain,
Though it's been years now since I left it,
Around my heart that string's still wound,
But now I'm just stuck in the real world,
With a wilted clover crown.

~e.h

Untied

When I was both young and naive,
I believed in anything,
And you told me that the twinkling stars,
Were tied up by a string,
That the moment I had joined this earth,
A brand new one was strung,
And every night out there in space,
My sparkling star still hung,
As it rose I'd ask the wise old moon,
Which star up there was mine,
Guessing at which point of light,
My life had caused to shine,
But nights are not eternal,
Nor naivety or youth,
And the world was quick to tell me,
What I'd thought was not the truth,
It wasn't string that stopped the stars,
From falling from the sky,
And you didn't get to untie yours,
When you kissed this world goodbye,
But I think there's always some things,
That pure knowledge can't explain,
And I'll stick to what you told me,
Though the world thinks me insane,
For it's hard to say what isn't true,
And see clearly which things are,
When on the night you slipped from earth,
I saw a shooting star.

~e.h

21

The Meddling of Minds

I once had a mind of quicksand,
That dragged ideas into its depths,
Inhaling specks of sunlight,
Every time I drew a breath,
But the world thought me a hazard,
When every word I spoke, I meant,
So around me they put caution tape,
And filled me with cement.

I once had a mind of tree roots,
Using the lack of light to thrive,
Discovering it's in darkness,
That we learn to feel alive,
But the world thought me too tangled,
That my mind reached far too wide,
So they ripped me from the earth,
Where constant sunlight left me dried.

I once had a mind of storm clouds,
With every lesson I grew tall,
Until I'd finally seen enough,
To let my observations fall,
But the world trapped them in buckets,
Before they could taste them on their tongue,
For surely minds are shallow,
When they belong to someone young.

~e.h

You reached in through my ribcage,
Snapped my heart strings one by one,
So their song will never sound as sweet,
As the first time they were strummed.

~e.h

Standing Still

It was the longest night in winter,
When I sent a question into space,
Asking how I'd ever change,
When I'm trapped in the same place,
And I heard the full moon giggle,
As she cloaked me in her light,
Along with the same swath of stars,
I looked at every night,
I blushed pink as a sunrise,
At the joke I didn't get,
Until the moon gave me her answer,
In the minutes before she set,
"You have much to learn on standing still,"
She told me with a smile,
"For since you first asked me that question,
You've moved five hundred thousand miles."

~e.h

Young Explorer

When you were young and scared of nothing,
You were enchanted by the moon,
And a field of glowing stars that clung,
To the ceiling of your room,
You drew lines to link their beauty,
Made constellations of your own,
An explorer of the universe,
With your warm bed for a throne,
And you remember one cold evening,
When those stars had lost their light,
How you grabbed your favourite sweater,
And padded out into the night,
And the sight that lay above you,
Made your tiny heart start reeling,
As a sea of glinting starlight danced,
On the world's now darkened ceiling,
But though the stars strung high above you,
Claimed you were part of it all,
You couldn't stop their large expanse,
From making you feel small,
For despite all of the lines you drew,
The constellations stayed the same,
And every star you made your own,
Already had a name,
But listen young explorer,
For a star's light can be slow,
And the ones you see above you,

Were made a long long time ago,
And though the world won't see it,
Until this earth's a lot more worn,
The moment that you saw that sky,
A brand new star was born.

~e.h

Wind and Waves

Their words spun like a cyclone,
Howling through the dark of night,
Promising acceptance,
If you gave up all your light,
But block your ears my darling,
You are not a brittle stone,
This storm cannot erode you,
For you're more than blood and bone,
You're deeper than the ocean,
Both unstoppable and free,
And nothing can control,
The wild intentions of the sea,
So when they try to shape you,
Slip like water from their palms,
For wind should know it's reckless,
To disturb the ocean's calm,
You have the right to be here,
Every right to what you feel,
And the wind can howl forever,
But the ocean will not kneel,
So do not let them change you,
Send your waves out far and wide,
And let them learn the hard way,
That you can't command the tide.

~e.h

A Postcard from the Moon

I am sending you this postcard,
From the dark side of the moon,
So you know I got here safely,
And that I will be home soon,
For today I held our planet,
Between the fingers on my hand,
And learnt there's more stars out here,
Than our earth has grains of sand,
So now the life I ran from,
Doesn't seem like such a wreck,
When the town that I grew up in,
Isn't more than just a speck,
And although my life feels tiny,
As I look back at our home,
I've realised we're the only ones,
Who don't live it alone,
That sometimes even shooting stars,
Send pieces down to earth,
When their solitary beauty,
Starts to cost more than it's worth,
I am sending you this postcard,
From the silence of the skies,
To remind you that there's beauty,
In our microscopic size,
So I hope next time you feel alone,
The moon shows you you're not,
And how lucky we all are to find,
Our home on this blue dot.

~e.h

Silence

If you've listened close to silence,
I'm sure that you have heard,
The gentle constant ringing,
In the space between two words,
When you really pay attention,
You find it's not just in your head,
But instead is whispers of the words,
The world has left unsaid,
It's "I love you" left unspoken,
And a mother's last goodbye,
That she never had the chance to say,
As she watched her daughter die,
It's forgiveness never given,
And a "sorry" left too late,
That would have saved a best friends life,
If they'd known it could not wait,
It's a phrase that could have helped them,
And it's secrets that could heal,
It's words from those too scared to say,
The truth of how they feel,
But you have an advantage,
For you're still alive to speak,
Words that could help save a life,
Or give strength to someone weak,
So may you never leave unspoken,
Words the whole world ought to hear,
Before they just become the ringing,
In another person's ear.

~e.h

<u>Be</u>

Do you hear them ask the sun,
How it learnt to burn so bright?
Or beg the stars to share the secrets,
Of the art of peaceful nights?
The know you cannot learn,
How to become deep as the sea,
For beauty can't be taught,
It happens when you simple be.

~e.h

Wayfaring Traveller

We're all wayfaring travellers,
Trudging down our separate roads,
Hoping, wishing, praying,
Someone will come to share our load,
There's sunburn on our shoulders,
And there are blisters on our feet,
We brave the wildest blizzards,
And the scorching summer heat,
Sometimes we find somebody,
Who is going our way too,
And while they walk beside us,
The sky seems a brighter blue,
But all roads twist and turn,
And when you reach an intersection,
It's likely life will take them,
In the opposite direction,
But don't give up on hoping,
When your road is a dead end,
It's likely that you'll find,
It's only really just a bend,
And though other's roads are different,
It doesn't mean that yours is wrong,
So pick yourself back up again,
And just keep trudging on.

~e.h

The Tug of the Tide

She told me that the ocean,
Had been calling out her name,
When the tide went out each evening,
She felt like she should do the same,
The waves tugged at her ankles,
As they pooled around her feet,
Whispering of wonders,
That she still was yet to meet,
But every time I asked her,
If she knew the reason why,
She simply said this arid world,
Had turned her deep heart dry,
There was just one way she knew of,
To finally feel like she was free,
And it was 14 000 feet,
Beneath the cold and stormy sea,
Then early in November,
She slipped like water from our hands,
Left nothing of her salty breath,
Or footprints in the sand,
And I hope she found the ocean,
Made up for things this world had lacked,
For she left a note to say goodbye,
And then never came back.

~e.h

My Message in a Bottle

There's a message in a bottle drifting from the rocky shore,
And it's a letter to what's next from everything that came before,
Inside its glassy walls is all the proof that I was here,
And it holds my whole existence as I watch it disappear,
I know it isn't easy to survive the stormy sea,
For the ocean's not forgiving to a tiny drop like me,
But still I beg the wind to guide it safely on its way,
As the sun kisses the water to salute the end of day,
While the memory of me fades with every minute that will pass,
The legacy I leave behind is trapped inside that glass,
And since there's every chance that it will never reach the shore,
I hope that bottle shares my life with all of the sea floor.

~e.h

Rainstorm

You were born to be a rainstorm,
To send your voice throughout the night,
To sing your song with falling raindrops,
To break the darkness with your light,
You were born to show raw beauty,
To wash the dirt out from their eyes,
But the whole world ran for cover,
When you opened up your skies,
So you made your thunder silent,
And learnt to bite your rainy tongue,
You gave them what they thought they wanted,
You gave them life with endless sun,
But as they watched their lives grow weaker,
Watched as their leaves turned brown and dry,
They wished they didn't take for granted,
Your booming presence in the sky,
You were born to be a rainstorm,
To be chaotic and be bold,
To show there's beauty in the knowledge,
That you cannot be controlled,
Because you might think you're not needed,
Life without you is the same,
But nothing beautiful would ever grow,
If it wasn't washed with rain.

~e.h

Shipwrecked

My heart's a lonesome island,
Disaster lines its shipwrecked shore,
A fleet of souls that thought they'd found,
What they'd been searching for,
But your treasure maps were lying,
There's nothing gold beneath my sand,
Don't let the sea convince you,
That it's safer on my land,
You might be a skillful sailor,
With nothing but the purest aim,
But I have fought so many pirates,
That you now all look the same,
So take heed of my lighthouse,
Even waves break on my rocks,
There's a reason not a single ship,
Has made it to my docks,
And I wish I could offer shelter,
From those storm clouds in my sky,
Because you've not made it ashore,
But you should know, neither have I.

~e.h

She longed to sit on the horizon,
Where the skyline kissed the sea,
For if the sun could hide behind it,
Then maybe so could she.

~e.h

Hopeless Dreamer

I've lost my heart, have you seen it?
Fumbled between the butter fingers of a boy I once loved.
Down,
Down,
Down it fell,
Into an ocean of long lost love,
Too weak to swim against the tide,
Until it's washed up and spluttering on my doorstep,
Begging to take its place in my empty chest once more,
And whispering,
Like all the hopeless dreamers whisper;

"Let's do it all again."

~e.h

Matter

You may not believe in magic,
But don't you think it strange,
The amount of matter in our universe,
Has never slightly changed,
That all which makes your body,
Was once part of something more,
And every breath you ever breathe.
Has seen it all before,
There are countless scores of beauty,
In all the things that you despise,
It could once have been a shooting star,
That now makes up your thighs,
And atoms of forgotten life,
Who've long since ceased to roam,
May now have the great honor,
To call your crooked smile their home,
You may not believe in magic,
But I thought that you should know,
The makings of your heart were born,
Fourteen billion years ago,
So next time you feel lonely,
When this world makes you feel small,
Just remember that it's part of you,
And you're part of it all.

~e.h

Our Weary World

If you go outside at night,
After the world has gone to sleep,
You can hear the planet sigh,
Under the secrets it can't keep,
And the wind sings different tunes,
To all the ones you hear by day,
As though it's choking on the words,
That we're all too afraid to say,
And I wonder at the problems,
We've tried to melt inside its core,
Whether it's packed so close to bursting,
That it can't hold many more,
For how can we see its weakness,
When we've not known something so strong?
And if it weeps and we can't hear it,
Does that mean there's nothing wrong?

~e.h

Your blindness to my downfall,
Has gone too far to be a joke,
As a stand ablaze before you,
And you tell me you smell smoke.

~e.h

Life Cycle

When it comes my time to sleep,
I will not wail, I will not weep,
I'll lay my weary body down,
On beds of leaves both green and brown,
I'll sleep as nature takes its toll,
Reclaims my once embodied soul,
And wraps me in the earth's embrace,
A quiet, peaceful resting place,
The time outside will still elapse,
But I won't feel my bones collapse,
And I'll return back where I came,
To let the cycle start again.

~e.h

Sunshine

She wove golden rays of sunshine,
Into a long and flowing dress,
That left the scent on everything she touched,
Of nature's sweet caress,
Everywhere the girl did go,
The flowers would all bloom,
And she could chase the lonely feeling,
Out of every darkened room,
She could drive out all your sadness,
And cause a frozen heart to thaw,
She'd paint the sky pink every morning,
But nobody ever saw,
No one thought to thank her,
For the warmth upon their skin,
Or for chasing all their demons,
From where the night-time's breath had been,
So she thought she wasn't needed,
She could leave and they'd not care,
But they'd just taken her for granted,
Since her light was always there,
Because you never thank the ground,
Until you know how it feels to fall,
Or just how much you need the sun,
Until it doesn't rise at all.

~e.h

The moment she stopped faking happy,
When she realised she wasn't 'alright',
Was when the sun always rose in the morning,
But her world stayed as dark as the night.

~e.h

Hope

You tell me that you're hopeless,
You want your life less than your death,
But if you jumped into a pool right now,
I know you'd hold your breath,
So I know that it's not hopeless,
But that your hope's just hard to find,
And if I showed you all you can become,
I know you'd change your mind,
You might have hit rock bottom,
But it's the perfect place to start,
Where the only thing that you can hear,
Is the beating of your heart,
You have to almost lose it,
To remember what you've had,
And that there's been a share of good times,
Mixed in between the bad,
So don't wait for the ending,
Until your last breath starts to leave,
Before you finally remember,
Just how much you like to breathe.

~e.h

I Love You Too

You said you couldn't keep waiting,
For me to say, "I love you too",
But I'd said it to you every day,
In ways you never even knew,
It poured over the umbrella,
. That I held for you in rain,
Caught in the way I kissed your bruises,
Just to take away the pain,
Baked in the cake I made you,
When you got the biggest slice,
And when you told me that you loved it,
How I baked it for you twice,
It was buckled in the seatbelt,
I always told you to put on,
And in the ways that I would miss you,
Every time that you were gone,
I might not have said those four words,
In the old and standard way,
But I'd learnt actions speak much louder,
Than anything that you can say,
So if you're really tired of waiting,
For those four words to leave my throat,
All I can say is that it's cold outside,
So don't forget your coat.

~e.h

The Tree of Unrequited Love

Her love spread out like branches,
Reaching upwards to the sky,
Giving shade throughout the summer,
And a place to keep you dry,
So all the city's children,
Built a tree house round her spine,
And though they never asked her,
She still told them she was fine,
They etched their names with knives,
Along the edges of her bone,
A handwritten reminder,
She was always theirs to own,
Despite the pain they brought her,
Upwards she still grew,
Thinking if you love someone,
It's the least that you can do,
But as the kids turned into adults,
And the winter air grew cold,
She wept sap from their carvings,
For they weighed too much to hold,
And the men all thought her branches,
Were to help their fires start,
And without a single "thank you",
Put a chainsaw through her heart.

~e.h

When you find yourself in darkness,
With just the thoughts your mind invents,
Is it scarier to have them at all,
Or that they're making sense?

~e.h

Names

You could never pronounce my name right,
In your mouth it sounded wrong,
Like a piece that tries so hard to fit,
But doesn't quite belong,
But I learnt to love it that way,
It was the only flaw you had,
Like you'd taken who I thought I was,
And changed it just a tad,
You'd whisper it in silence,
Or shout it through the air,
A reminder that the love I'd found,
Was nothing short of rare,
Before long you got tired,
Of my name's unpolished sound,
And I watched it slip right off your tongue,
And shatter on the ground,
My name once full of loving,
Is just a broken syllable,
And now when people say it right,
I don't react at all.

~e.h

Surrender

Five hundred words of steel,
Shot like bullets from your throat,
Punching holes through all the good things,
That I used to stay afloat,
Dark black water laps beneath me,
I can feel its gurgling breath,
Waiting for the perfect moment,
To drag me down into its depth,
But maybe there is freedom,
In feeling things I had denied,
So I lay down in its icy arms,
And surrender to the tide.

~e.h

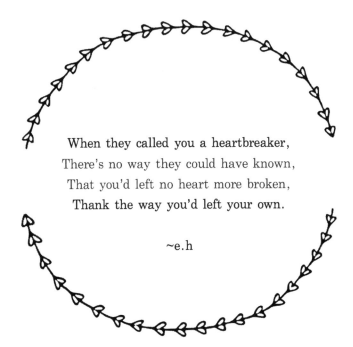

When they called you a heartbreaker,
There's no way they could have known,
That you'd left no heart more broken,
Thank the way you'd left your own.

~e.h

Sickly Sweet

He fed you sweet sweet words like honey,
Their taste like sugar on his tongue,
No one had ever been so kind,
So to every word you clung,
He told you you were pretty,
In the dress that he had bought,
That you were smart when you remembered,
All the things that he had taught,
You came to need those words,
Just as much as you need air,
The way they showed that you had beauty,
Ever since he'd placed it there,
But you didn't see the truth,
The holes the words left in his teeth,
As he used all of the sugar,
To coat the rotted heart beneath,
He revealed to you your beauty,
But made it so you would believe,
That you'd be quick to lose it,
If you ever were to leave,
So you stayed stuck fast beside him,
As you fell deeper for his trick,
Smiling like nothing was wrong,
When the sugar made you sick,
But let me tell you something,
You do not need him there to shine,
A boy should never have a say,

On how your worth's defined,
I know you have the power,
To break out of his sticky grip,
For you were beautiful before the words,
Had touched his sour lips.

~e.h

Shattered Starlight

She had stars behind each eyelid,
And a galaxy in her soul,
That drew people to her endless heart,
Like the pull of a black hole,
She was made of earth and fire,
Of wishes cast on shooting stars,
She was a brand new solar system,
Unlike the ones they'd known so far,
With constellations ever changing,
No one could memorise her skies,
And they thought the thing for them to do,
Was bring her to their size,
They shrunk the universe within her,
Told her her vast expanse was wrong,
That she should make her life much smaller,
If she wanted to belong,
As they collapsed her world around her,
She felt her inner stars grow cold,
Until her life was far too heavy,
For her once strong arms to hold,
You might wonder how it happened,
But I guess that it makes sense,
Because a life becomes much heavier,
When it's the universe condensed.

~e.h

Mother Nature

Have you heard of the girl with the sun on her skin,
Who can make flowers grow with her light from within?
And she runs through the world leaving life in her wake,
With blossoms all lining the path that she takes,
She must be quite shy for she's never been seen,
But she's what paints the grass such a rich shade of green,
I've heard people say that there's dew in her veins,
That whenever she's hurting or lonely, it rains,
And if you listen on nights that are early in spring,
You might just hear her voice on the breeze as she sings.

~e.h

Beau•ti•ful *(adj.)*

You tell her that she's beautiful,
She laughs and asks you how,
When there's a crack on her front tooth,
And there's a crease between her brow,
Where is all the beauty,
In her slightly-too-big nose,
In the freckles on her cheeks,
And how her hair takes years to grow?
And you wonder where she learnt,
That beauty lies upon your skin,
So that she thinks it doesn't cover,
Everything she holds within,
Its very definition,
Is "*pleasing to the sense or mind*",
But she's let them change the way,
She thinks her beauty is defined,
It breaks your heart to know her mirror,
Is how she estimates her worth,
And not the lives she's made much better,
By simply being on this earth.

~e.h

Origami

She folded her life like origami,
Made what was large into something so small,
Bending and creasing her edges,
Until she filled almost no room at all,
She'd learnt to always say sorry,
That she was a burden for taking up space,
And so into herself she was folded,
Locked in her own suffocating embrace,
The world tore at all of her edges,
Once sharp corners had started to fray,
Now so tiny that nobody noticed,
As she slowly began to decay,
Reduced to just ashes of moments,
The wind swept her up off the floor,
And her pieces were scattered in places,
She'd not dared to inhabit before,
As her eyes took in all of the beauty,
Of a world which she'd lived life deprived,
She learnt there's no need to say sorry,
Taking up space simply means you're alive.

~e.h

Supernova

They witnessed her destruction,
Then were left to wonder why,
She saw nothing but darkness,
Though the stars shone in her eyes,
But maybe they'd forgotten,
When they failed to see the cracks,
That a stars light shines the brightest,
When it's starting to collapse.

~e.h

The Way It Is

It was just past her fifth birthday,
When she learnt to search for truth,
And she questioned every thing she learnt,
From then, right through her youth.

She asked **who** had decided,
Only boys could play in dirt,
But her mother said she didn't know,
And straightened out her skirt.

She asked **what** time the sun set,
So she could walk home in its light,
Because she'd heard it's far too scary,
To be on the streets at night.

She asked **when** they would teach her,
What the whistling calls all meant,
But they said she should feel flattered,
It was a type of compliment.

She asked **where** the saying came from,
That "Oh, boys will be boys",
And why there wasn't one that told them,
That "Girls are not your toys."

She asked **why** he'd still done it,
Despite her endless stream of no's,
Why the words she spoke meant less to him,
Than what lay beneath her clothes.

But they said she had the habit,
Of asking far more than she should,
It doesn't really matter,
If the world's not understood.

So she never asked the question,
How they could say that she was free,
When she'd forgotten who she was before,
They said who she should be.

~e.h

Brown

You hated your eye colour,
Called it a dull and dirty brown,
Wished for the deep blue of an ocean,
Where admirer's hearts would drown,
And it pained me when I realised,
You'd never see it like I do,
The way your eyes hint at a story,
That I want to read right through,
They hold specks of stolen sunlight,
That you'd miss with just one glance,
And a depth of raw emotion,
That can freeze you in a trance,
They're a fix of melted chocolate,
When I'm craving something sweet,
But hold a gaze that's so unwavering,
That I find it hard to meet,
I fall right down the rabbit hole,
When I look into your eyes,
The brown of earth's unfettered beauty,
That I yearn to memorise,
When I was tired of not belonging,
They made me feel like I'd been found,
And I hope you never say again,
That your eyes are simply brown.

~e.h

The Burning of Bridges

I see your figure from across the valley,
Head down as a sign of defeat,
Hands clenched on the times you were happy,
Body sweating from the intense heat,
The flames are now high as your kneecaps,
Their movements reflect in your eyes,
Still easy to see from this distance,
That it takes all you have not to cry,
I could send you my voice on the breezes,
But my throat is determined to choke,
Not sure if it's stuck on emotion,
Or smothered in all of this smoke,
You yell out that I should just leave you,
You'll be better once you are alone,
These fires will fight the dark winter,
That threatens to freeze all your bones,
But the cold's not the reason I'm worried,
Nor the clouds that are heavy with rain,
It's the fact that you'd rather be burning,
Than admit to the world you're in pain,
And the hurt that will come when you realise,
Once to ashes the flames have been turned,
That there's no warmth in a fire born solely,
From all of the bridges you've burned.

~e.h

Not My Favourite Song

I remember when we realised,
Our favourite song was the same,
I felt like you had looked at me,
And seen straight into my brain,
You'd stroke my face while singing,
As I drifted off to sleep,
And I swore that those fond memories,
Were the kind I'd always keep,
But even good songs finish,
And as the winter's silence grew,
My cheeks went from a rosy pink,
To a mottled black and blue,
So I grabbed the person I'd become,
And fled into the night,
You told me that I'd come back,
And you still think you'll be right,
But let me tell you something;
Our song was on the radio,
But it's been so long since I've heard it,
I've forgotten how it goes,
And I've learnt it takes just seven years,
For all your cells to be replaced,
So one day you will have never touched,
The skin upon my face.

~e.h

Change

I once heard someone say,
If you don't change you do not grow,
But I waved the thought away,
For who were they to think they know,
I'd always stayed the same,
A heart that thrived within the cold,
And I had no desire to change,
At least that's what I had been told,
But deep within my mind,
A thought grew slowly, bit by bit,
Until I felt trapped in my skin,
For it no longer seemed to fit,
There's a whole world sitting out there,
Changing every single day,
That proves it's nothing to be scared of,
If you do it the right way,
For a day afraid to turn to night,
Will miss the silver moon,
And a flower that refuses change,
Will never get to bloom,
I had thought I was a thorn bush,
Only good for snagging clothes,
But if you do not dare to change,
You'll never find out you're a rose.

~e.h

There will come a day I know it,
When you'll love yourself as I love you,
And you won't view your scars as ugly,
But a tally of times you made it through.

~e.h

The Attic

There was a creaking in her attic,
The kind that settles in your bones,
Makes your heart flee when you have the thought,
Of facing it alone,
Her mind made it an object,
With each creak sending her numb,
Like the noise possessed a pair of hands,
Wrapped tight around each lung,
The world told her to fear it,
"There's nothing good in the unknown",
And she wondered if they'd ever faced,
The creaking of their own,
So she built herself a ladder,
From the thoughts that screamed to stop,
And she climbed it to the darkness,
Waiting at the very top,
There inside her attic,
Prepared to fight it to the death,
Her fingers shook against the switch,
And fear gripped at her breath,
As the light flickered above her,
Not a monster was in view,
But a group of dreams she'd dared not have,
In fear they'd not come true,
The creaking in her attic,
Had been a plea into her heart,
A dare to face the unknown,

And release them from the dark,
Because you won't encounter freedom,
If you give in to your fright,
Sometimes the bravest thing you'll ever do,
Is just turn on the light.

~e.h

6am

Don't cry because he told you,
That his love has slipped away,
Because I once knew a boy,
Who watched the sun rise every day,
One morning I sat with him,
Wrapped entirely in my awe,
But he said he'd viewed so many,
Six a.m. was all he saw,
And you're a brilliant sunrise,
With your darkness-breaking light,
But I know that he's forgotten,
Life without you is just night,
He cannot see your beauty,
Since he's taken it for granted,
But that doesn't mean it's failed,
To leave the rest of us enchanted,
So I promise someone's out there,
Who'll watch you rise over again,
And they will never come to see you,
As just another six a.m.

~e.h

Missing You

I missed you for too long,

in too many ways,

that it became just another part of me;

engraved deeper into my heart with the passing of time.

I would wake up,

stretch,

breathe,

and miss you.

They told me to let it go,

to let *you* go,

and I would say:

You cannot simply will your heart to stop beating,

that no matter how long you hold your breath for,

you cannot hold it forever,

and I could only stop missing you,

if I stopped being myself entirely.

~e.h

Holding On and Letting Go

I was the type of person,
That held onto things too tight,
Unable to release my grip,
When it no longer felt right,
And although it gave me blisters,
And my fingers would all ache,
I always thought that holding on,
Was worth the pain it takes,
I used to think in losing things,
I'd lose part of me too,
That slowly I'd become someone,
My heart no longer knew,
Then one day something happened,
I dropped what I had once held dear,
But my soul became much lighter,
Instead of filled with fear,
And it taught my heart that some things,
Are not meant to last for long,
They arrive to teach you lessons,
And then continue on,
You don't have to cling to people,
Who no longer make you smile,
Or do something you've come to hate,
If it isn't worth your while,
That sometimes the thing you're fighting for,
Isn't worth the cost,
And not everything you ever lose,
Is bound to be a loss.

~e.h

Highway of Happiness

I got lost on the highway of happiness,
Took a wrong turn on the road of regret,
And I found myself walking through memories,
That I'd been trying hard to forget,
They grew out of cracks in the sidewalk,
Found their way up the bricks of the walls,
With thorns grown so sharp that they promised,
To pierce my young heart should I fall,
These memories spread endlessly outwards,
Until they were too far away to be seen,
But as I bent down to study some closer,
I found something nestled between,
There tucked beneath all the brambles,
Were memories I'd long since forgotten,
Pieces of proof that my lifetime,
Wasn't just made of things that were rotten,
These flowers had slowly been growing,
From the moment that I had been born,
But they'd almost lost sight of the sunlight,
When I'd only remembered my thorns,
And as I stumbled back onto the highway,
I knew there was much more to learn,
But in a world that is fearful of failing,
I was glad that I made a wrong turn.

~e.h

Burn

She threw herself at heartbreak,
Like a moth drawn to a flame,
Patching up her broken wings,
Just to try it once again,
And the world all thought her foolish,
For she never seemed to learn,
But how do you save somebody,
Who's convinced that they should burn?

~e.h

Without

You said there was no beauty within you,
You were a candle devoid of a spark,
So you set all your feelings on fire,
In the hopes it would light up your dark,
You said there was no beauty within you,
You were an ocean whose depths had run dry,
So you filled all the cracks in your laughter,
With a flood of the tears you would cry,
And I wish that the beauty within you,
Hadn't caused you to view life with doubt,
Because you said there was no beauty within you,
But there sure is no beauty without.

~e.h

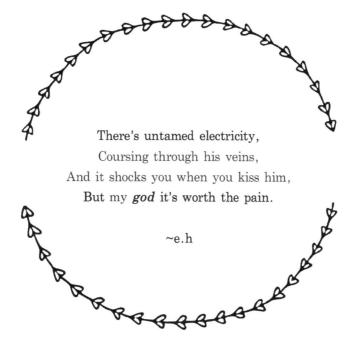

There's untamed electricity,
Coursing through his veins,
And it shocks you when you kiss him,
But my **god** it's worth the pain.

~e.h

People Are Not Poetry

You can write for hours on hours,
Of all the things that you wish you could be,
But the truth of the matter is simple,
People are not poetry,
And I know that you wish you weren't awkward,
That sweet words could roll right off your tongue,
But your time here's too short just to worry,
How each single sentence is strung,
It's okay to be rough round the edges,
To be bruised up and broken and scarred,
But it's not okay to let people tell you,
That it's a reason to change who you are,
Your hair doesn't always sit neatly,
The way a poem sits so neatly in lines,
And sometimes you might feel like a word,
That nobody has learnt to define,
You might not be a star that lights darkness,
Or a bird that can teach us to soar,
But it's okay, because you are too complex,
To be crammed into one metaphor,
It's okay not to know what you're doing,
Since your feelings don't have to all rhyme,
Though a poem once complete is eternal,
You have the freedom to change over time,
You're much more than can ever be written,
There is no title to say, "This Is Me",
You can't be trapped in the lines of a notebook,
Because people are not poetry.

~e.h

Picture Perfect

I was obsessed with "picture perfect",
I searched the world inside and out,
For a single moment I could say,
Is what life's all about,
My life was viewed through lenses,
My camera a medal worn with pride,
I thought it held the moments,
That I'd always keep inside,
But looking back at photos,
I can't remember how I felt,
The noises that the world made,
Or the way the warm air smelt,
I don't remember how the day was,
If it was going good or bad,
I've just a snapshot of a moment,
That nobody even had,
So I gave away my camera,
And now use my eyes instead,
To take photos for the scrapbook,
That I've made inside my head,
I always thought my photos,
Were ways to make my moments last,
But you remember life much better,
When you don't view it all through glass.

~e.h

Spring

Life is unpredictable,
It changes with the seasons,
Even your coldest winter,
Happens for the best of reasons,
And though it feels eternal,
Like all you'll ever do is freeze,
I promise spring is coming,
And with it, brand new leaves.

~e.h

Thumbelina

They called her Thumbelina,
She was small but very wise,
Fit in the tiniest of places,
Due to her peculiar size,
She would listen to your secrets,
Laying nestled in your hair,
Give your thoughts much needed company,
When you thought no one was there,
With your tears large as an ocean,
She would catch them in a cup,
Worried what would happen,
If you ever used them up,
To her you were an artwork,
She painted freckles on your nose,
And sewed a little love,
Into the size tag on your clothes,
When you looked into a mirror,
Too caught up in what you lacked,
You never saw her sitting,
On your shoulder, looking back,
And it led you to started thinking,
No one was there for you at all,
She tried to tell you she was,
But her voice was far too small,
So you spent your life not knowing,
When you thought you were alone,
That the hole you had in your heart,
Was the exact size of her own.

~e.h

A+

They announced it on a Monday,
In our school's old sweaty hall,
That a girl that I had math with,
Wasn't coming back at all,
You could hear the silent questions,
She was perfect wasn't she?
What demons was she fighting,
That we were all too blind to see?
I sat in math that Monday,
Beside her now abandoned desk,
While our teacher warned us not to fail,
Our fast approaching test,
I remember she once whispered,
That she was envious of me,
My parents knew the work it took,
Just to get a simple 'B',
I wish I'd noticed earlier,
Or had the decency to ask,
Because her world must have been crumbling,
Behind her "perfect student" mask,
And I wonder if on that Sunday,
It was the last thought in her brain,
That the only A+ she could give,
Was the blood type in her veins.

~e.h

Unspoken

There's a history of heartbreak,
Tucked in the creases of her eyes,
A museum of the moments,
That she'd watched just pass her by,
And each tear that escaped her,
Held the things she'd left unsaid,
So the words she'd never spoken,
Stained her dampened cheeks instead.

~e.h

The Liar and The Thief

She was a liar and he was thief,
Suspended inside different stages of grief,
When nobody listened despite how she sung,
She learnt to twist truth on the tip of her tongue,
His pockets were laden with diamonds and keys,
So no one would notice the blood on his knees,
They lived worlds apart but one thing they both knew:
"I'm fine," sounds the same even when it's not true.

~e.h

Puzzle Pieces

Our lives are one big puzzle,
We don't know how many pieces we've got,
There are people that fit in quite nicely,
And people who try but do not,
We're constantly adding more pieces,
All the memories of things we've been through,
We add laughter and tears and adventure,
And the lessons we've learnt to be true,
Everyone has their own puzzle,
There will be ones where you do not fit,
Don't you ever dare make your piece smaller,
Just so you can live there for a bit,
If you keep cutting off all your edges,
One day you won't recognise what you see,
And you'll forget the person you once were,
Before the world told you who you should be,
Make the most of each piece in your puzzle,
It'll be a grand masterpiece when it's done,
So you won't have to look back when it's over,
And realise you've left out the sun.

~e.h

Breathe

Her touch was as light as a feather's,
She drifted through life as a pocket of air,
Every move that she made went unnoticed,
A breeze the only slight sign she was there,
Nobody acknowledged her presence,
And it wasn't until she had started to leave,
That people would instantly wonder,
Why it became so much harder to breathe.

~e.h

Swordfight

I said I was a writer,
Then saw scheming in your glance,
You had wished to live forever,
And now I was your chance,
You clawed your way inside me,
Shot jet black ink in through my veins,
Made sure that I would write of you,
Until I drove myself insane,
You longed to be the hero,
Like in the books you used to read,
Remembered as the kind of the man,
That everybody needs,
It was too late when you noticed,
The one mistake that you had made,
That a warrior might fight with swords,
But the pen's a writer's blade,
You can't just tear my world up,
And then expect a loving rhyme,
You used your words as sharpened weapons,
And now I will use mine,
I trapped you in ink handcuffs,
Locked you behind my written bars,
And now you'll finally live forever,
As the monster that you are.

~e.h

Glass

You warned me we're all made of glass,
That our lives are far too thin,
So why did I not believe you,
'Til it was your shards in my skin,
Now these scars upon my fingers,
Run too deep to just forget,
Despite the wilted roses,
From the first time that we met,
And I don't know why I told you,
I was good at letting go,
For all I do now's watch dead flowers,
And pray somehow they will grow.

~e.h

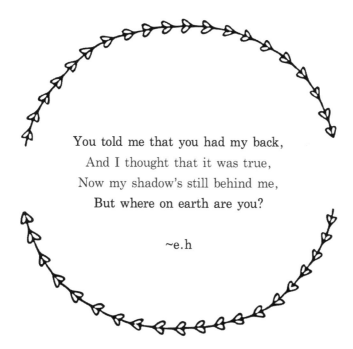

You told me that you had my back,
And I thought that it was true,
Now my shadow's still behind me,
But where on earth are you?

~e.h

Heartbeats

She bought things with her heartbeats,
Dealt in the currency of time,
Counted her pulse to track her spendings,
While she waited in long lines,
She wasn't one for banking,
Heartbeats aren't something you can save,
You either spend them or you lose them,
Until you're lying in your grave,
She'd give heartbeats to strangers,
While she listened to their woes,
Because a heart's worth more than money,
As far as money goes,
She splurged heartbeats on moments,
On afternoons with age-old friends,
Who asked how she was happy,
Without a dollar she could spend,
But money only buys you things,
While heartbeats buy much more,
They buy you loud side-crippling laughter,
That leaves you rolling on the floor,
Heartbeats buy you moments,
They buy you tears and hugs and smiles,
They buy you time to reminisce with friends,
You haven't seen in quite a while,
Money can't buy heartbeats,
And that's a fact you've always known,
So make sure each day you're happy,
With the way you spend your own.

~e.h

Air

She was a silent fighter,
With a demon in her lung,
That stole her breaths right from her,
Before they'd hardly passed her tongue,
He was a silent fighter,
Who was always taught to share,
And held his breath when he was with her,
Just so she could have his air.

~e.h

She sprouted love like flowers,
Grew a garden in her mind,
And even on the darkest days,
From her smile the sun still shined.

~e.h

Soul Sharers

I remember when the world broke in,
To rip apart my soul,
For years after that one event,
I thought myself not whole,
My hours were spent with trying,
To fix it up with tape and glue,
Until one day I discovered,
Everyone else was broken too,
Here we were with pieces,
Of ourselves in both our hands,
So fragile and so open,
That I began to understand,
Maybe I'd been greedy,
To want my soul all to myself,
When it could be a lot more helpful,
In the palms of someone else,
Now every time I go somewhere,
I leave part of me behind,
And collect all of the pieces,
Of others' souls that I can find,
So when I'm meeting someone new,
It's not just me they get,
But also tiny fragments,
Of all the others that I've met,
And my life's become much bigger,
Now that it's home to things so small,
And if this is what "broken" means,
I do not mind at all.

~e.h

Life

Life can be the sunshine,
On peaceful days with bright blue skies,
Or life can be the raindrops,
That fall like tears squeezed from your eyes.
Life can be the heaven,
That you'll only reach through hell,
Since you won't know that you're happy,
If you've not been sad as well,
Life can teach hard lessons,
But you'll be wiser once you know,
That even roses need both sunshine,
And a touch of rain to grow.

~e.h

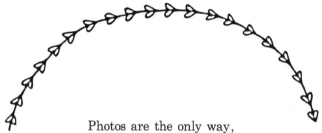

Photos are the only way,
To hold on to what you knew,
For the moments they show never change,
When the people in them do.

~e.h

There is freedom waiting for you,
On the breezes of the sky,
And you ask, "What if I fall?"
Oh but my darling,
What if you fly?

~e.h

Made in the USA
San Bernardino, CA
12 June 2017